SIGMUND FREUD

THE FOUNDER OF PSYCHOANALYSIS

THE HISTORY HOUR

HISTORY

CONTENTS

PART I

INTRODUCTION

The book you are about to read should enlighten you to many things that you never knew about *Sigmund Freud*. The real issues in *Freud's* life and how bad it was for others. How unfair it was to all others that had the unfortunate chance to cross paths with him.

It is hard to believe that one man who is such a sexual deviant could have become so famous in his lifetime.

The book will introduce you to some of his unorthodox methods that you will be able to tell immediately cannot be real. For example: take a bone out of someone's nose to stop their menstrual bleeding.

It will allow you to see the rise and fall of *Sigmund Freud* and make you wonder what wires had gotten so crossed and so frayed in his brain to make him into the insane person he became to do everything he had done.

PART II

GOLDEN SIGI

«I cannot think of any need in childhood as strong as the need for a father's protection.»

Sigmund Freud

≈

Sigmund Freud was the first child and son of his father who had been twice widowed and was on his third marriage. *Sigmund* was born in Freiberg, Moravia which is now called the Czech Republic on May 6th, 1856.

≈

Sigmund's mom, *Amalia Nathanson*, was only nineteen when she married *Jacob Freud*, who was the age of thirty-nine. *Jacob* had two stepbrothers that came from his dad's first wife and almost the same age as *Sigmund's* nineteen-year-old mother. *Sigmund's* stepbrother had an older son, making him *Sigmund's* nephew and *Sigmund's* earliest and first playmate.

It caused *Sigmund* to grow up in a weird family dynamic with his mother nearly half the age of himself and his dad. Seven children were younger born, but it did not matter, *Sigmund* was always his mom's favorite child.

When *Sigmund* turned four, his family moved to Vienna, Austria; the capital of the Austro-Hungarian monarchy which had become the complete rule in Central Europe in Hungary within Austria during the time of 1867 – 1918. *Sigmund* would always live in Vienna except for the year before he died.

The *Freud* family were all Jewish, and *Sigmund's* first experiences were that of some outsiders walking into an overwhelming full Catholic community. The Jews of Austria had been liberated, which gave them rights equal to and allowing all of them to settle where ever they liked in the empire.

Several Jewish families came to Vienna the same as the *Freuds* during 1860. The professional and educational opportunities were much better than what was in all the provinces as well as being a higher standard of living. The *Freuds* lived in an area where there was a high concentration of other Jewish people. The area was called the slums of Leopoldstadt.

It seemed all the housing was cramped and that the *Freuds* were always moving. Sometimes they were living with *Sigmund's* father's family. When *Sigmund* was ten years old, his family had increased so much that he had one brother and five sisters.

Sigmund attended the local elementary school. All of *Sigmund's* family realized he was brilliant of mind from the very beginning, and even though they had a four-bedroom house for eight people, they let *Sigmund* have his room while school was in session.

Sigmund was most parent's nightmare and lived with them until he turned twenty-seven years old because that seemed to be the custom during that time.

Sigmund's father *Jacob* had never been very bright or successful in business. The importance of Freiberg had been declining, and the young *Freud* family left and then eventually decided to settle in Vienna, Austria.

Sigmund's father was a dealer in textiles. His first marriage was when he was seventeen, and from that marriage, he had two kids: Philipp and Emmanuel. He became a widower but remarried in either 1851 or 1852 to someone named Rebecca. It is hard to find out much about Rebecca, and it is not known if she died quickly after marriage or if she was repudiated. He again married for a third time to another young woman who was twenty by the name of Amalia Nathansohn (1835-1930), and her firstborn was *Sigmund*. He was followed by Julius that died at eighteen months, Rosa, Dolfi, Alexander, Anna, Mitzi, and Paula.

Sigmund did inherit his dad's sense of humor, skepticism before life's doubts, the habit of demonstrating with a Jewish story when he wanted to bring to light some moral of the story, his free thoughts or liberalism.

It seemed that *Sigmund Freud* had taken his "*sentimentalism*," from his mother and that he was capable of having intense emotional feelings.

Freud delighted in all the love and attention his mother, Amalia doted on him with and called him her "*golden Sigi*." The unconditional seemed to make *Freud* figure out that when you are the favorite kid of your momma, during your entire lifetime, you keep the feeling of being a victor, you always keep feeling successful, through reality seldom seems not to fulfill.

When *Freud* was eight, there came upon him another less pleasant memory that would play a role in a dream of victory later, which the dreamer interpreted himself. When he remembered it and discussed it, he felt humiliated and inferior before his parents.

What is the story? It seems his dad would scold him because he peed in his parent's bedroom on purpose. His father said that *Sigmund* would never amount to anything. *Freud* feels that what his dad said should have caused him mental issues because that dream scene kept repeating itself and was always associated with the counting of his successes and works. It was like *Freud* was saying that no matter what his father had said about him he had still become someone.

Another memory grieved *Freud*, and that was when his dad had taken him for a walk, and a rude by-passer made a comment to *Sigmund* for him to get off the sidewalk because he was a Jew! *Freud* was hurt and disappointed when he realized his dad had not reacted when the stranger had insulted him, *Sigmund*.

PART III

FREUD'S EDUCATION

«Most people do not really want freedom, because freedom involves responsibility, and most people are frightened of responsibility.»

Sigmund Freud

Freud started at a preparatory school called the Gymnasium and remained the top in his class for seven years. He graduated '*summa cum laude*' and at that time had decided to made medicine his specialty. Due to this, it led to a variety of many exclusive privileges, some that required him to need to take any of the necessary examinations.

Because his grades were so excellent, it allowed him special privileges at home. It did not matter what *Freud* wanted, and it did not matter how bad the family's finances were. As *Sigmund* got ready for college, he at first thought about studying law. But when he learned of Darwin's ideas on evolution and listened to Goethe's article on nature, he had decided by then to go to a medical student.

Freud started studies at the University of Vienna in 1873. At first, he was discriminated from the discrimination and prejudice since he was a Jew. *Freud* felt that he was expected by those discriminating him to feel inferior and no good since he was a Jew; it did not matter; he kept putting one foot in front of the other. It helped him for later in life to be prepared to deal with all the resistance that would occur as people would respond to *Freud's* theories.

Freud's initial research project at the time he started medical school and upon the suggestion of Professor Claus. That professor had been interested in a study conducted by a Polish scientist by the name of Simone de Syrski who had supposedly found the structures that seemed to represent the male eel's testes. It was a question that everyone had been trying to answer for centuries and without any success.

Four hundred eels had been dissected, and *Freud* seemed to confirm the findings of Syrski's. It appeared the research was never definitive, and *Freud* almost no satisfaction when the work was published. It did not matter to *Sigmund* because he was about to gain satisfaction while in the laboratory of the physiology of Ernst Brucke.

Ernst had become a renowned anatomist, physiologist, histologist, and even more. *Freud* developed a great respect for Brucke, who became his new mentor. *Freud's* research that was conducted with Brucke's oversight was definitely impressive.

About this time, Brucke decided to put *Sigmund* working on the study of the anatomy of the human spinal cord and all its neurons. The structure of neurons during that time was nowhere understood. *Freud* took it upon himself and modified his histological methods of staining that were being utilized in the laboratory. He developed what was called a gold chloride technique to stain the nervous system tissue about the year 1880. It was to be one of the first time the use of heavy metal stains were utilized on nervous system tissue. There had been a method to stain neurons that had been developed by Golgi in 1873.

In 1878 *Freud* had decided that he would change his birth name from *Sigismund* to *Sigmund*. It was in 1881 that he would graduate with his full doctorate in medicine. It would not be until 1888 that Cajal would first report on the brain's structure using the Golgi technique.

The research that Golgi and Cajal did share the Nobel Prize in 1906 for Medicine. If *Sigmund* had not left the research to make his career in medicine, he could have ended up famous at that time.

Eventually, *Freud* left the university and started his career in the medical field at General Hospital there in Vienna, Austria. A big reason for leaving and to begin his career of medicine was because he had met his *Martha Bernays*, the lady who would one day become his wife, and he needed to start making money so he could support a family.

Before all of this, he must establish his career and medical practice. At General Hospital, he worked and met with Theodor Meynert, who was first to suggest correctly abnormal functioning of one's basal ganglia was the cause of Parkinson's disease.

Freud's interest was stimulated in brain function and anatomy, so in 1891, he wrote and published a book *"On Aphasia."* You might remember that there ntwo main speech centers in your brain, and they are called Broca's area, which is speech production, and Wernicke's area, which is speech reception. If there happened to be damage to either of the regions, it would result in either Wernicke's aphasia or Broca's aphasia.

If you happen to read *Freud's* book written on aphasia, you will find he was very critical of Wernicke. Both men wound up smack in the middle of an argument on functionalism vs. structuralism as it would pertain to the human brain activities. Meynert thought and even suggested that *Sigmund* needed to start studying the anatomy of the human brain. *Freud's* real interest was in the diseases of one's brain.

By the recommendation of Brucke, *Freud* was given a Fellowship for Traveling, and this allowed him a paid trip to Paris so he could study at the prestigious Salpetriere. He had wanted to study under one Jean-Martin Charcot who was '*one*' of the more famous neurologists in the world at the time, and the gentleman who gave the name to Parkinson's disease after one physician; James Parkinson.

PART IV

COCAINE – A GREAT ADDICTION

«The doctor should be opaque to his patients and, like a mirror, should show them nothing but what is shown to him.»

Sigmund Freud

Freud had a youthful but enthusiasm toward cocaine, but he sure liked to use this excellent drug he '*said*' for treating his wounded and admired friend, Fleischer.

The treatment seemed to have been a total disaster for Fleischer, who wound up in a psychosis caused by the cocaine. During the time *Freud* was all caught up in the study of his dreams, he started struggling by working on a much larger project while working on the writing of "*The Interpretation of Dreams.*"

It seems there is a particular interest when it comes to the episode of cocaine use in *Freud's* life. For an explanation, it appears that you will find it lying in the fact that cocaine falls into the group of substances that are prohibited by law today and the sensation vendors can imagine *Freud's* use of cocaine that might reveal his shocking but outrageous private secrets.

Sigmund for sure had his weird personality, and it continues to hold a fascination to this current day. Even more to a more significant extent than any of his work, but the public interest is not as determined through a justifiable desire by knowing mostly the hope in discovering a few of the elements that are so sensational by the master's biography.

People can imagine that if they could see an episode of cocaine use in *Freud's* everyday life, it could undoubtedly be the indication of the '*drug-addicted*' *Freud*. But, on the other hand, there seemed to be a need to demolish some of the great personalities by using a decisive influence with the western culture is almost irresistible. Therefore, the care for any biographical specifics that could prove and be an active backing to this one unique need.

Freud's personal friendship with cocaine seemed to not satisfy either the biographical details of the slanderers or gossip mongers. The following might give you an idea of a particular aspect of his cocaine friendship.

The truth, the real truth; *Freud* was a flat out cocaine user, and in today's time would be called an addict. But, you see, cocaine was not illegal during *Sigmund's* time. Instead, it was being prescribed as a euphoric. Absolutely! Even now, there has been no harmful side effects discovered to cocaine. If you only think back to the famous Coca-Cola beverage as it contained cocaine extract, and it was quite telling and very addictive. The cocaine addiction itself and the harmful effects have only been discovered lately.

Freud liked using cocaine for its stimulating effect, something that would help him in managing his depression. For *Freud* to achieve that level of well-being, a '*high*' you might call it, and still be able to relax under tense circumstances.

There were medical advantages with cocaine for *Freud* as well. He began his researching in the field as it concerned the impact of using cocaine as a medicine, for minor surgery to be exact.

He gives away about himself, on the adventure or experiment if you will, whatever you desire to call it as he wrote in his biography. In 1884 he had a deep interest and made *Freud* have the drug company Merck supply him with the alkaloid that we knew little about at the time so that he could study its physiological effects on others.

When *Freud* was totally engrossed in the research, there was an opportunity for *Freud* to make what he considered a critical trip to see his fiancé, who he had not seen in person for at least two years. *Freud* quickly then completed his investigation with cocaine as seen in the short article he published. He noticed that there would be other forthcoming substances that would soon be revealed.

During the very same time, *Freud* made an intense recommendation to Konigstein who was his friend and an eye doctor, so they could check the extent of the effects about the anesthetic cocaine qualities if used around one's sore eyes.

When *Freud* returned, he found that another one of his friends, Carol Koller, after hearing the news about cocaine, had started conducting experiments on the eyes of animals' and was able to present his findings when at the Ophthalmology Congress held in Heidelberg, Germany. For that reason, Koller had been considered rightfully as the real discoverer about using cocaine-based anesthesia to be used locally, which had become essential for minor surgery.

There was a Vienna magazine that carried the article about *Freud's* "*On Cocaine*" in the year 1884. He gave the detail of Koller's having become so knowledgeable in the field of cocaine was probably due to the following reason.

Freud had accidentally run into one of his old colleagues who had been complaining about abdominal pain, so he recommended for him to take a cocaine solution of 5% and this caused the patient of complaint to start feeling numb in his lips and tongue. Koller was there and witnessed the entire event; so *Freud* was sure it was at this time when Koller noticed the anesthetic qualities of the drug and stole the ideas and published an article as if he had discovered the use of cocaine.

It seems odd, however, that with *Freud* being so close to gaining the status of a scientific celebrity by publishing his findings of this miraculous drug cocaine. However, it still could not shroud one tragic event that he never mentions in his biography.

In *Freud's* research for the effects of cocaine, it was all for his own, personal reasons. He had hoped he would be able to help a good friend by the name of von Fleischl-Marxow; someone that had become addicted to morphine, to help soothe the pain he was being afflicted by due to an infection.

Bad went to worse when the cocaine prescriptions he gave his friend proved fatal. *Freud* would be the one to exclaim in 1885 that if the cocaine could have only helped his pain. One would wonder why *Freud* would not be wondering why his friend had died! The patient died a painful, slow death, and what remedy had been used but proved to do nothing but make his suffering much worse. Marxow had turned into a cocaine addict, just like he did with the morphine, and had to keep raising the doses of the cocaine to get relief. He died seven years later when he was 45 years old.

Identified later was by using the cocaine while withdrawing from the morphine was the trigger to cause the downward spiral into an agonizing death. At the end of the works, it was noted that the properties of cocaine to produce localized anesthesia would in the future come to be used for anesthetizing the cornea for surgery.

Sigmund was not only the father of psychoanalysis. He was one of the leading medical advocates for cocaine. His favorite test subject being himself. It seems that *Freud*

decided to kick his cocaine habit about the time of his dad's death in 1886. During that period, he had written a letter that said that the next time he wrote them, it would be more transparent and in better detail, and incidentally, that cocaine brush has lain to the side.

PART V

HYSTERIA & HYPNOSIS

«The conscious mind may be compared to a fountain playing in the sun and falling back into the great subterranean pool of subconscious from high it rises.»

Sigmund Freud

Charcot and his clinical using of hypnosis for his attempt in finding some organic cause for the hysteria that caused *Freud's* interest to be aroused in the psychological neurosis causes. He did revise his results partially later, but they seemed to have a significant influence on the psychoanalysis and psychiatry of his one student, *Sigmund Freud*.

Freud had studied with Charcot in August 1885. When he did successfully establish his hoped-for creation, the psychoanalysis, when considered as an independent type of science, can often be forgotten as beginning with Charcot's study of hypnosis.

∿

There is other research regarding Charcot's altered states of consciousness that was caused by a hypnotic trance that seemed to produce other disciples that were now less conformist to a materialist period than even *Freud's*.

∿

When you are talking about the field of hysteria and hypnosis, Charcot can be remembered for all of his work on his patient Louise Gleizes, that helped increase his fame during his entire lifetime.

∿

In the beginning, Charcot thought that '*hysteria*' had to be a neurological disorder, and the patients had to be predisposed by their hereditary features showing from their nervous system. Toward the end of his life, Charcot had decided that hysteria was a psychological disease.

∿

During the 19th century Charcot seemed to be the representative of ruling science. He had come to terms with hypnosis, trying to find an explanation for neurophysiological for all the symptoms he had observed. He wanted to look for an explanation that was purely materialistic for those people that he could hypnotize easily and even be considered as someone who was mentally ill. It explained the different levels of hypnosis that could be easily defined and classified.

It so happened that Charcot held the position of representative of ruling science during the 19th century. He had finally come to his position on hypnosis, and he worked to try in finding an explanation for the neurophysiological symptoms he was observing.

He wanted to find an explanation about why the people that could be so easily hypnotized might be considered to have a mental illness. If so, could those people be strictly classified by the consecutive hypnosis stages?

There were two physicians who in 1884, started to question this theory. It was Amboise Liebeault and Hippolyte Bernheim that put the theory forward that the hypnotic state that was being produced purely by suggestion had finally been proven in the medical practice of Liebeault.

What was realized was that Charcot believed that being hypnosis seemed to be caused by a disease-related cause was due since he had worked on the Salpetriere and mostly with hysterics. Charcot himself finally admitted defeat a few months before dying when he announced in an article that when one suffered from hysterics are usually easily prone to suggestion.

～

Charcot found two different kinds of hysteria, major and minor. The interest in hypnotism and the hysteria seemed to have developed at the time when everyone had become fascinated with *'mesmerization'* and what was called *'animal magnetism.'*

～

Charcot went on to argue strongly against the sincere belief of popular and medical prejudice, so you rarely found hysteria was seldom seen in men; if so, when seen in the male population it was usually a traumatic case of hysteria.

～

The analysis by Charcot, mostly his view on hysteria was an organic condition that could be brought on by trauma and paved the path for toward understanding the neurological symptoms that came up from war-related and even industrial-accident wounds.

～

The doctor, Jean-Martin Charcot that had been so interested and gifted artistically since youth even collected the historical descriptions of hysteria. Charcot presented photography for a method to clinically document on the one hand and then as an academic method for teaching on the other.

Charcot himself died after a seizure of angina pectoris in 1893 when he was 67 years old. It is the same with so many writers, philosophers, and doctors who were working toward the end of the 19th century. It was at this time that *Freud* became increasingly interested in those patients who were unconscious. *Freud* felt that the unconscious was a dimension of a human life that was once important and inaccessible for a source of actions and thoughts.

In *Freud's* effort to decrypt some of the meanings of the hysterical symptoms and the other mental phenomena that was neglected which seemed to be beyond the control of conscious (like slips of the tongue and dreams), this caused *Freud* to move further from his training in neurology.

Freud stayed true to his commitment that the idea which seemed meaningless in behaviors would be expressed the unconscious conflict. It enabled him to develop the techniques to determine what the reactions could mean.

Sigmund traveled to Paris so he could study with Charcot in

1885; where Charcot was documenting the different stages of hysteria by using photography.

The practice was suspicious since patients seemed to tend to play act or perform in front of the camera, and the doctors did record those who were most photogenic. *Freud* did devote his time to studying hysteria, but at least he tried to avoid making the symptoms with his patients worse by making them eager to perform.

There was a rival of Charcot's by the name of Bernheim became convinced that the hysteria seemed to be the product of one's suggestion and it was possible that it be treated by hypnosis. *Freud* did support Bernheim in his attempt in making hypnosis and suggestions legitimate subjects to question for science so that they could be developed as therapeutic devices. One patient; Bertha Pappenheim which we will call the Anna O. case for the medical history. (1859 – 1936).

When Anna O. described the traumatic experiences and all the feelings she had about them to Breuer, it seemed she started getting some relief from her debilitating signs and symptoms like her partial paralysis and the haunting hallucinations.

Breuer's treatment had not been as successful as Breuer and **Freud** had publicly claimed. Pappenheim did finally overcome the symptoms she had and went on to be an inventive social worker along with being a leader in Germany in the women's movement.

By using hypnotic suggestions, the doctor could command his patient to stop having or developing the symptoms. By free suggestion, the physician anticipated on creating the conditions that the patients would be able to grasp the meaning of the symptoms they had and be able to free their selves from their illness.

But then we must look at if it was free association; how free was it? Did the psychoanalysts still try to use their suggestions even if they did not give any commands to their patients?

We will now look at "*The Rat Man*," case where **Freud** tells us of a young attorney that had been plagued by manias that involved torture, rats, and some forms of punishment. Rat Man's obsessive thoughts and acts were then traced to his inconsistency about his father and sexuality.

The symptoms were manifesting his ambivalence even

though they were covering it up at the same time. *Freud* had his original medical notes on this case have been found the most comprehensive that ever existed. He wrote the raw medical records into a form that could be published to serve the purpose of proving his theory. It did sometimes exaggerate the effects of getting beneficial treatment and even the duration.

'*The Wolf Man*,' is a medical case history was a wealthy aristocrat of Russia, who seemed to be suffering from fears and compulsions that were causing his sexual development to go haywire to the point of being debilitating at a very early age.

Freud had the "**Wolf Man**" focus his attention on a dream from childhood that seemed to capture his current fears and his early traumas: it was a dream about wolves who were perching up in a tree located outside his opened bedroom window. The doctor worked with '*Wolf Man*,' so they could discover what wish the dream was disguising.

All through his career, *Freud* would consider how it was that an analytic interpretation could be helpful to the patient, and how he could prove it to be true. How could the interventions of each analyst differ from the hypnotist's suggestions?

Freud wrote an essay late in life where he again returned to the same question of how the influence of each analyst and the construction, insight, interpretation, and memory could be related to each other.

It seemed that no matter what, *Freud* tended to sneak in some sexual implication in all of the impossible and possible contents of each dream.

Freud always seemed to use the theories of "*transference/change*" and "*counter-transference/counter-change*" in referring to any strong emotions the patient presented toward the doctor or in some cases the doctor toward the patient.

The transference could be like treating the analyst like your father to promote therapeutic works, but *Freud* also knew that this might mess a patient's head up for sure perspectively.

Given one analysis could seem successful to you entirely because it seemed that way and it felt right, *Freud* and even his critics were wanting to know precisely how they could determine if the results were a real insight. The particular influence of the doctor-patient emotions on the analysis does play a leading role in two of the cases.

Dora had been sent to *Freud* in the year 1900 and was suffering from what seemed like "*hysterical*" symptoms: depression, nervous cough, and not being sociable. Dora, a teenager, had been trying to resist the love interests and advances toward her by a family friend; the husband of a lady that Dora's dad was having an intimate affair with.

Instead of trying to interpret the hysterical symptoms and what they meant to Dora, *Freud* persisted they had to have significance with his theory toward sexual roots that hysteria required. Dora did like this diagnosis and rejected *Freud* and all of his ideas and thus left the treatment program.

Freud started treating a poet in 1933 who said to him that she wanted to equip and fortify herself so she could face the war when it did come. *Freud* and his patient both shared a strong passion for mythology and archaeology. For both of them, Athena, who was the Greek goddess of warfare and wisdom, it seemed to carry a special significance.

It was in 1937 that *Freud* asked how one would know when

analysis (treatment) should end. The analyst and the patient would then decide to stop appointments. Did that mean then that the patient had no more unconscious conflicts left over in their mind to discover?

Freud, in one of his '*pessimistic*' essays, emphasized that no matter what the unconscious conflicts would always be there and could still cause substantial problems.

Hysteria by itself, is considered psychoneurosis, by which your unconscious conflicts appear emotionally as a severe mental disorder or with physical symptoms (which some doctors will call a conversion reaction), is not found to be dependent on any known structural or organic pathology. The underlying anxiety can be assumed to 'convert' over to a physical symptom.

The word comes from the Greek hysteria, and that means "*uterus*." A "*wandering uterus*" theory can reflect an ancient notion that one's womb could become moved around into different positions.

Because of this, hysteria was put off to be a female disorder and attributed to that malfunctioning uterus. Hysterical symptoms can develop in males or females and are most common in young adult life.

~

As the end of the 19th century was approaching, Charcot, demonstrated some morbid ideas that could produce some physical manifestations.

~

He had a pupil by the name of Pierre Janet, who was a French psychologist who emphasized the psychological instead of the physical causes of hysteria.

~

It would be later when **Freud** started investigating with Breuer about the psychic methods that were involved in hysteria and had developed this theory that it had been brought on by emotionally charged memories that had been repressed by the patient.

~

Cases described in the 19th-century of classical hysteria are now rare. In our modern times, most of the psychoneuroses seem to be in "**mixed**" forms where the hysterical symptoms can be found throughout other types of neurotic disturbances.

~

Those motor or sensory expressions of hysteria seem to be delegated conversion type reactions since the disturbances will generally no follow any anatomic pathways of the nervous system.

Sensory Disturbances

Might include the senses of hearing, smell, vision, or taste; and can range from some weird sensations by hypersensitivity for complete anesthesias; it involved the experiencing of severe pain that there was no organic cause identified.

Remember that motor symptoms might vary from complete paralysis to contractures, convulsions, tics, or tremors. If there is loss of speech, nausea, hiccuping, coughing, vomiting are at times hysterical in their origin.

The attacks of sleep-walking and amnesia are considered to be emotional dissociative reactions.

PART VI

FREUD & FAMILY

«We are never so defenseless against suffering as when we love.»

Sigmund Freud

≈

Sigmund Freud in 1877 was for sure an ambitious 21-year-old that planned on devoting his entire life to science. Or, that was the way it was until he met the love of his life, and that turned all his plans upside down.

≈

Martha Bernays Freud was born in Hamburg July 26th, 1861 and passed from this earth in London on November 2nd, 1951. She was **Sigmund Freud's** wife; he is the Austrian psycho-analyst.

Martha happened to be the second daughter of Berman and Emmeline Bernays. Her dad's grandfather, Isaac Bernays had been a Chief Rabbi of the city of Hamburg, Germany. *Sigmund* and Bernays met during April 1882. They were engaged for four years and finally wed on September 14th, 1886 in Hamburg.

Bernay and *Freud* sent love letters during the four engagement years, according to *Freud's* official biographer who had read all the letters felt the letters would be worthy of being contributed to some of the excellent love literature that existed in the world.

To their marriage, they bore: Daughter Mathilda (1887-1978), Son Jean Martin (1889-1967), Son Oliver (1891-1969), Son Ernst, (1892-1970), Daughter Sophie (1893-1920), and Daughter Anna (1895-1982). *Freud's* dad, *Jacob*, passed away in 1896.

Freud laid down the foundations for modern thinking when it came to families, relationships, and sex, but when it came to his own life, well, it was mostly ignored.

There is now some new research that sheds light on the woman that stood behind and supported *Sigmund Freud*, the strong, hard-headed wife, Martha. She was undoubtedly a woman who was ahead of her time. *Freud's* greatest inspiration and shared his addiction to cocaine, but not the same appetite for sex. She said the reason he was a psychoanalyst. But turned around and said his work was nothing but "*pornography*."

There is a book to be published about *Martha Freud* of the biography coming from a publisher in Germany, which will detail her entire life and will tell about her when she ended any sexual relations with *Sigmund* after they had their sixth child, and realizing she still influenced *Freud*.

By examining the hundreds of letters that had been written between them and other evidence from diaries, records, and surviving family members; it is believed if *Freud* had not run into Martha and fell madly in love; he would have made a more significant mark in his career as a scientist who perfected how to use cocaine in medicine.

Freud, who was one of the very first to begin working with cocaine by experimenting on himself and may I mention again; he liked it very much. He said it gave him energy, lifted his move, and because he was so excited about it he would send packets of it to Martha, and he told her it would make her cheeks have more color.

∿

Freud had noticed how well the cocaine worked as an anesthetic and planned to experiment further on the properties, but it did not matter, his concentration then was all on romancing Martha. While he was away with Martha, one of his colleagues picked up on the cocaine studies and became famous and made a fortune. *Freud* was to have said that having 53 years with Martha was worth it all.

∿

Research shows *Freud* being a '*cold appraiser*' of any human behavior. *Freud* was a romantic and passionately jealous. *Freud* fell in love at first sight with his beloved Martha.

∿

Martha, coming from a strict orthodox Jewish family, had been expected to marry someone better than *Freud* who was nothing but a penniless atheist and had no position in society. They kept the fact they were engaged a secret for as long as possible.

∿

Martha's mother moved all her daughters to Hamburg from Vienna, and this began a four-year separation for the young lovers who saw each other only about a dozen times.

Sigmund was so jealous that he told Martha in one letter that he forbid her from being able to ice skate because she might glide around on the ice arm-in-arm with some other man.

Martha tried to pass her time by helping around the house she lived in with her sister and mother. Martha loved the theatre and reading. Her interests in all the arts were upsetting to *Freud*, who felt as him being a scientist that he had no weapons against any artists. He felt all anyone had to do was write some song for a woman and '*boom*' they held the key to the lady's heart.

It seemed there was no real prospect of making a good living from scientific research and *Freud* being so desperate to marry his Martha; he made a very painful decision. Thus, only six months after meeting Martha, *Freud* decided to give up on his scientific research and become a doctor.

After *Sigmund* had advanced in his medical career enough to make Martha's mom happy, Martha moved to the city of Vienna, and they were married. It was at this same time that *Freud* was causing trouble and scandal. He was talking to the women folk about sex, and that was taboo in that day, let alone anyone writing about the female liking sex or fantasizing.

Freud spent three years being so lonely working at Vienna General Hospital. He tried internal medicine, surgery, and psychiatry and still not knowing what he wanted for his specialty. *Freud* rarely saw Martha, and he pined for her. *Freud*, being so restless, read Goethe, Shakespeare, and Cervantes late into the nights and then every date he would write long, romantic letters.

Martha was just the type of wife that *Freud* had wanted; she was busy with the family and the house. The next nine years, she stayed pregnant all the time and gave birth to their six children. She raised their little family of children and oversaw the household as *Freud* would attend to his practice and still research his medical theories.

The domestic duties seem to take over, and the passion between *Freud* and Martha had for each other in the beginning. They still settled comfortably in their routines of each day of life. *Freud* was consumed by his work, but all the ardor and longing had gone by the wayside in their marriage.

Freud seemed to be thriving in his atmosphere of strength and the order in his home. It seems he was the one who needed the firm foundation so he could explore the timeless world regarding the unconscious. As *Freud* dug deeper into all the mysteries of sexuality (level of sexual activity) through his research, so the passion faded out in his marriage.

Every Sunday, their family would gather in their house. *Freud* would come out at noon, and he would put his two fingers out and squeeze each child's cheeks as it was his sign of affection. He never hugged anyone, just squeezed cheeks.

Freud, after being married for ten years to Martha, had found he was established as the patriarch of his own family. His exhaustive work in trying to find a cure for problems with hysteria had never brought him any fame, happiness, or success that he had wished for so long. The fear of child-hood of poverty kept resurfacing a haunting him.

When *Freud's* father, eighty-year-old *Jacob* died on October 23rd, 1896 in Vienna after suffering from a four-month illness; *Freud* was shaken deeply.

It seems that *Freud's* feelings about his father dying were confusing and complex for him. It seemed he felt that he had replaced his dad in his mom's affections as a child. Trying to understand the real nature of hysteria, he could only imagine that his dad had been abusive to him and some of his other siblings.

Freud was only a little boy when he had it figured out that he was his mother's favorite and *Jacob Freud* was his rival – and he had won. It can be as hard as if you lose, to win over your dad can cause you a great deal of guilt, especially after you die.

By self-analysis, *Freud* could see the truth about the relationship with his mother and father. He came to identify that his dad was indeed innocent. He also came to know that when he was a little boy, he had wanted to be able to marry his Mother and felt his Dad was the rival for his mother's love.

Freud already knew that his wishes were the same among every boy in every culture. He even gave the new phenomenon he had discovered the name of Oedipus Complex, and could one day be found as one of the utmost but essential ideas.

After *Jacob Freud* died, *Sigmund* began working on a book that had been based on some of the results coming from his dreams and the self-analysis of them. His Interpretation of his Dreams it would be known later would put *Freud* on a pedestal as one of the most highly revered minds during his time, and it brought him even more fame and wealth that his dad would have ever been able to imagine. It would be later before *Freud* revealed his motivation behind the book that he would feel was the most famous book he had ever written.

Freud felt it was a part of his self-analysis, and it told of his reaction regarding his dad's death – so the most important thing that had happened in his life was the loss of another man's life.

The fall of 1891, *Freud* was barely scraping by enough so they could move into a new to the heart of Vienna to an apartment. It would be five decades he would call this place his home. In the small office that connected to the apartment, he could see his patients and still do the work that could bring to him the fame he always seemed to crave and felt would be his.

His granddaughter, Sophie, said his work was the priority over everything in the house. She also mentioned that he led a traditional lifestyle; he wanted their home organized at all times. Their meals were at an exact time and on the hour. The entire household had to build its schedule around his. In the family, there was never anything casual. It was all very formal, and it was in a structured society.

Freud had regular habits, and they were the same all the time. His barber was the person who trimmed his beard and mustache. He would stroll down the boulevard every day, play cards with his same friends each Saturday night. He was extremely conscious of how he looked and was all the time dressed to the fault. Most of all, he loved that good cigar, and he smoked more than twenty of them a day.

PART VII

ANNA, O.

«The mind is like an iceberg, it floats with one-seventh of its bulk above water.»

Sigmund Freud

∽

Wilhelm Fliess (1858 – 1928) seemed to play a significant role in the preparation of psychoanalysis. He was from Berlin and an oto-rhino-laryngologist; Fliess happened to meet *Freud* on Breuer's prompting after he had attended a few of his conferences there in Vienna.

∽

The two of them developed a strong friendship bond. Fliess became the moral supporter and confessor for *Freud*, and during the time that *Freud* was the most productive and working as a psychoanalyst and they exchanged letters.

It turned out that Fliess was more than just an audience and critic of all *Freud's* ideas. He had some ambitious contributions towards science that begged for *Freud's* approval. Fliess was the author on a theory of the reflex nose neuroses, and it included the assumption of vital periodicity and bisexuality.

A latter theory, which is a kind of biorhythmology stated all vital processes; even the ones that included pathological can develop into a cycle that lasts 28 days with women and 23 days with men. It would have been helpful to determine the various numerical dealings that could have been helpful to decide on how much time for recovery after the disease, and the possible date for somebody's death.

For the most part, the direct influence of Fliess on the beginning of psychoanalysis is usually considered unimportant. Fliess seemed to be the first one to pull *Freud's* interest to the jokes most significant as the most valuable part of the material for the psychoanalytical research. *Freud* declared that it was the others who taught him that there was always something considered accurate behind each favorite fantasy.

The theory of bisexuality stayed where it was in *Freud's* essays when it came to sexuality that was published in the beginning 1900s.

The part that involved Fliess is more of a story about the projection of the ambivalence of the psychic in an instance with *Freud*. It is alright when you discover that unquenchable need to have an enemy or a friend; all rolled up in the same person. *Freud* seemed to have a lot from his confrontation with the scientific ideas that included some of his friend's insights into his emerging theories.

Most became acquainted with friendly and professional relationships that went on between Fliess and *Freud* when you read their letters that were preserved by Marie Bonaparte, during a time when *Freud* seemed to be in a great hurry to finally immigrate to Great Britain as friends along with his family in 1938. The correspondence between the two of them covered the period of 1887-1902, and it stays as a first-hand document for studying the development of the *Freudian* psychoanalytical thinking.

Anna O. that we spoke about earlier had been born on February 27th, 1859 in Vienna, Austria. Her family was Jewish and relatively privileged. Anna also had a brother younger than she, along with two older sisters. In 1867, Anna O. was eight years old, and her sister, Henriette, passed away from tuberculosis.

The society and times that Anna O. grew up in was a time that limited women the opportunities and she decided to leave school so she could take up the fun and leisurely hobbies like sewing, instead of resuming her education.

It was 1880 when Anna's dad caught tuberculosis, and Anna decided to devote herself in caring for him the entire time he was confined to bed. It was sad, but her dad's illness was terminal, and he finally died in April of 1881.

While he was sick, his daughter got sick too, but with different symptoms. Anna started consulting Josef Breuer for any signs that related to her being sick.

Freud had noted that before she got sick, Anna had been healthy and was an intelligent young woman with a dynamic mind and imagination, who daydreamed regularly and she worked on her household chores. The way she devoted herself to caring for those who were sick like her father had started taking a toll on her until there came the point when Anna was even kept from seeing her father.

Anna's illness seemed to develop in four stages:

Latent Incubation Period

Starting in July of 1880 and hanging on until about December 10th that same year, it appeared Anna's illness had begun. *Freud* said that with other patients, the beginning signs of this illness would probably not have been even noticed but those unusual symptoms he had seen with Anna did result in it being so visible by everyone else.

Manifest Illness

Symptoms seem to be their most severe. Anna started to recover, but in April 1881, when her dad passed on, it was the event that affected Anna very severely. June 7th, 1881, there was concern about her suicidal tendencies that caused her to be moved from the third-floor residence to live in a house in Vienna.

Intermittent Somnambulism

It was between April and the month of December in 1881 when Anna started switching between periods of sleep-walking and what seemed to be normal behavior.

Recovery

Breuer says that after he had finished his treatment with Anna, it took her a long time to recover that seemed to last until almost June of 1882.

Anna had such a wide range of symptoms that it made her illness even more confusing. It ranged from sleepwalking and cough to:

- Involuntary eye movements: it also included vision issues and sometimes a squint.
- Paralysis in her right leg and arm.
- Hydrophobia: she did not want anything to eat or drink, and that left her not able to drink anything for several days at a time causing dehydration.
- Difficulty with Language: Anna would be halfway through a sentence and then repeat the last word and then pause before she finished it. She started speaking in several languages, inclusive of her careers. No matter, Anna was not aware of what was going on, and it finally affected her so that she was not even able to talk for two weeks.

It took quite some time, but they eventually diagnosed Anna with hysteria, and so she spent most of her daytimes in a state of pure anxiety where she experienced hallucinations like those of skeletons and scary black snakes, maybe those being caused from seeing her hair.

In the day when she would wake up from a nap, she would be in a state of discomfort, tormented, and crying. When the sun went down, Anna would go into a deep state of hypnosis. *Freud* in his notes said if she could describe the hallucinations she had during the day while in her trance-like period for the evening, she could then wake up healthy and be able to spend the rest of her waking time in the evening more herself and at ease.

During some of Anna's therapy sessions, Anna was able to recall on one occasion when she had a glass of water and her nanny's dog, one she did not like taking a drink from the glass of water making Anna feel repulsed. This one traumatic experience alone probably caused her not to be able to drink water because Ann had somehow formed the association between the adverse event and water in her earlier life.

PART VIII

IT WAS EASY TO COVERUP THE WRONG

«The flowers are restful to look at. They have neither emotions nor conflicts.»

Sigmund Freud

～

Sigmund Freud carried out on himself a self-analysis in 1897 and made himself the 19th patient. He did reach one important conclusion and that he and his siblings did all show the same hysteria symptoms. It implied that they had all gone through sexual abuse when children. The mere idea was unthinkable at the least, and it was felt that *Freud* tried to play off his stories like they were fantasies so he could protect his family.

～

Freud avoided blaming the fathers at any costs. In *Freud's* cases, he wanted to make the abusers be the sisters, aunts, brother, governesses, uncles, but never the fathers. He went so far as to publish incorrectly one of his articles blaming the uncle of a 14-year-old girl as being the one who did the molesting, but then decades later she revealed it was her father.

Some believed that *Freud's* decisions were swayed by abusers that he knew personally. Fliess, one of *Freud's* best friends, even was a suspect in molesting his very own son.

Freud had confided in Fliess that he felt hysteria or any other psychological problems were from the child being sexually abused. After *Freud* found out that Fliess was one of the guilty who had abused, *Freud* felt he could not go on speaking about it and gave up all his theories and the evidence he had on sexual abuse.

Others spoke out against *Freud* and said he knew all about child abuse and its consequences that seemed so destructive, but he still suppressed the critical information and all the memories of rape to nothing but fantasy. It makes this author feels that *Freud* had at times been less than truthful about many things; so maybe he was not as smart as everyone had been led to believe.

Freud had grown desperate in trying to salvage what was left of his career and trying to gain popularity. He went so far as to make it normal for that despicable ritual where adults were '*initiating*' children to have sex and to pave the way for significant setbacks toward the feminist movement in that time. However, it also had an effect on the field of psych for many years to come.

Freud would dismiss females and their hysterias (basically PTSD that they suffered from caused by early childhood traumas) that led to some gaps in the research of PTSD that would go on and affect the soldiers involved in WWI.

Freud excommunicated anybody that tried to criticize the parents as far as abuse. By himself, he set back the understanding of child abuse as far back by at least one hundred years.

It seems that the Victorian age men were quickly able to hide their immoral and illegal sex practices. *Freud* seemed to only demand that sex should be practiced with the utmost discretion to ensure that the Victorians could keep their respectability. For any attempt in exposing a violator would only reveal their victim and the alleged sexual motives, that would stigmatize them even further; '*so keeping it a secret was the only course to go.*'

It is still happening today, that terrible stigma surrounding those traumatized about the sexual abuse, leaving the victims to think they are the ones that wanted, imagined, or deserved the abuse they received. The apparent lack of acknowledgment and dismissal of these traumatic events remain, and as long as we let *Freud's* legacy support, it could go on for several more years.

It seems odd that *Sigmund Freud* would develop his theory of seduction in 1895-1897, and then all of a sudden to abandon it. Like it was said and has been repeated over and over, *Freud* did abandon his first theory of neuroses and told this to Fliess in a letter that was dated September 21, 1897.

Recurrence and the relics of the entire theory are still grouped in *Freud's* work. What seems to be the most surprising in this fact is it had been tabooed and even misrepresented up until 1964.

It seemed that *Freud's* original theory on seduction was mainly confined to the area of psychoneuroses. It makes one think that *Freud* might have theorized that the existence of those unconscious for neurotics alone, and he promoted that this hope for the cure could come and mean the complete elimination of those unconscious.

The one theory sought and to explain the growth of the unconscious merely by cruelty, in the child, or sexual scenes and memories that were experienced while they were in the care of an adult.

Due to this fact, it brought in three consistent levels into play now: a topographical dimension, a temporal dimension, and then a language-related dimension. The temporal feature of seduction seemed to have been bound with the concept of the deferred action or even the "*afterwardness*," that was to survive throughout *Freud's* thoughts later.

While left in suspense, a person's initial memory then became traumatized and pathogenic when it was revived by a second scene occurring that had some association with the first occurrence.

The structural aspect of this theory on ego while it is still in its process of forming. It is armored against attack from the outside but no less against the attack from inside. Whatever attacked it the second time was not to be an outside event but a simple memory, the ego was not protected and was only able to react by repression.

And lastly, there was a linguistic side of the theory suggested through *Freud's* comparison that was between the barrier that separated those two moments of psychical trauma and then a translation, or even a partial failure of the translation.

It is pretty apparent just how inaccurate the response to reduce this seduction theory down to the simplistic claim that when the adult seduces the child, it can bring on the mental disturbance. One must realize then that *Freud's* first theory had to be woven into the clinical doctrine of that time.

When 1897 came to a close, *Freud* decided he would make a systematic critique of his theory that had led him to abandon it in the first place. It surrendered the hysterics to the "*seduction fantasies*," and the fantasies alone ultimately led to genetic determinism.

PART IX

MASTURBATION & PENIS ENVY

«The interpretation of dreams is the royal road to the knowledge of the unconscious activities of the mind.»

Sigmund Freud

While some researchers were trying to write a conjoined biography of the lives of *Sigmund* and Anna *Freud*, the very papers that were needed to be examined on Anna were kept locked in the *Freud* Archives. It took nine years in researching in a novel that was fact-based that was about Anna and how her life must have been growing up as a lesbian daughter of a man who at the time was considered a highly revered thinker who felt that lesbianism was the only access to mental illness.

Freud must have been an "*interesting*" father in several ways according to the novel.

- Even the great *Freud* had penis envy. When he was very ill and an old man with mouth cancer that was about to kill him, he still had surgery on his testicles to try and cure his impotence.
- *Freud* had always felt that "*short is better*." The idea had nothing to do with male genitalia or even cigars. It had to do with jokes. *Freud* loved good humor, and he wrote "*Wit and The Relation to the Unconscious*," which has some real merit as psychoanalytic theory, a joke book, and as an ethnography of humor.
- *Freud* seemed to get around as he had sister-wives. There was his wife, her sister Minna Bernays who had lived with them for years. Minna at one time confided tearfully to him about the affair she was having with *Sigmund*. After *Freud* died, Jung told the secret he had been protecting all along. The community of psychoanalysts had made fun of his claim and said it was because *Freud* had thrown him out of his inner circle. After four decades passed proof itself surfaced after Jung had died in a guest log from an Alpine Inn that had been found in 2006. Minna would travel with *Freud* a lot; his wife refused to go with him. The guest log revealed that Minna and *Freud* had checked into the honeymoon suite of the inn for two weeks. It was during this stay that *Freud* would write to his wife

Martha and complained that he and Minna had to try and make do in the two sub-par separate rooms.

- *Freud* had one joke that seemed right on par for him to have generated:

> *"A wife is much like an umbrella. Eventually, you will take a cab."*

- *Freud* did not mind telling others he was disappointed in his sons that were grown. Martin, the oldest, suffered from "*arrested development*," and he slept with so many women and so indiscriminately. Now, his youngest boy, Ernst, bless his heart, suffered from agoraphobia. Then there was his middle son, Oliver and their relationship that seemed to be compromised after there had been an encounter with Oliver when he was a teenager and *Freud* had gotten on to him,

> *"A real gentleman must not ever do these things, not even subconsciously."*

- There is not a record of what Oliver had done that had brought on the scolding.
- *Freud* sent Oliver to one of his friends to be analyzed. *Freud* knew he should never analyze a family member, but he still analyzed Anna, his daughter. With what everyone can come up with his clinical hours with Anna seemed to total up to at the least 1,000 clinical hours. Everyone would like to know what they talked about. All we do know is that

from a paper that *Freud* had presented to Congress two years after he had started analyzing Anna, "*A Child Is Being Beaten*." It seemed *Freud* and Anna discussed masturbation fantasies of Anna, ones where she had been beaten by one enraged father who appeared to be angry about an infraction that had never been her fault. Did it have something to do with Anna's lesbianism? No one knows for sure, but it is a good possibility. Anna lived to be 82 years old and stayed in the closet. She still spent the last 54 years with Dorothy Burlingham, the heir to the enormous Tiffany fortune. No one but knew anything but Dorothy's four kids knew the nature of the relationship between the two women. One of Dorothy's sons while on his deathbed did reveal that his '*two*' mothers had lived as spouses no matter how you looked at it.

- Charles Darwin-inspired some of *Freud's* theories. *Freud* seemed to be thrilled to imagine as humans we evolved from the apes. If this were the case and we had evolved from apes, maybe our emotional side had as well. The reasoning helped *Freud's* theory about the castration complex as a front of morality.

- *Freud* held to the belief that boys' seem to learn wrong from the right because of their subconscious racial memories when witnessing father apes while castrating their sons because of minor issues.

- *Freud* also thought that because girls had no protuberant genitalia for them to protect that girls would never be able to acquire the morality and would forever need guidance from their fathers and then later, their husbands.

- *Freud* also felt that the female opposite of the castration complex was penis envy. Once a girl realizes she does not have a penis, the maturing girl will begin to desire her dad's penis. When she does realize that she will not be able to procure him, she will want a baby. However, men seem to be predestined for some reason to grow increasingly moral while women will be predestined to connive and lie so she can get a man to impregnate her and then give this man moral guidance. Due to the lack of power from this husband, and that is what makes the lesbians fragile emotionally.

Freud had become a doctor when masturbation and lesbianism were both considered to be symptoms of '*hysteria.*' Many of the doctors would treat the hysteria with opiates, clitoridectomies, and ovariectomies. *Freud*, however, would only treat hysterical women by counseling with them. You had to give him a little credit as he seemed to urge all his patients to start looking inside themselves and celebrate at what they realized was there.

Even though *Freud's* like was fraught with the crazy details of his life and his theories sometimes seemed not to make any sense, it appeared his idea that when someone became physically ill, it could be caused by emotions as it was a remarkable discovery for humankind.

~

Freud always had a theory for everything, mainly those that related to females, and they certainly seemed to be misguided, and for sure misogynistic when we look at them now.

~

To *Freud*, one's compulsion to own firearms comes from one's unconscious need for compensating some deep-seated psychological sense of inadequacy and insecurity in terms of power. Men, mainly because they had a small penis or what the man considered a smaller-than-desired penis and with females, an attempt to somehow symbolically be able to grow a large penis.

~

During the Victorian age, all guns had been seen as objects of masculinity, and because of *Freud's* theories, their guns did symbolize their penis. Pistols served as a constant reminder that if a woman carried a gun like her dad, it might indicate that she wanted to be a man or even look at herself like she was a powerful type man. Or, if *Freud* looked deeply enough, it could have meant a woman carried a gun to shoot the men in her life, she could no longer stand that pushed her around. However, during *Freud's* earlier years, knives seem to be the weapon of choice for women.

PART X

FREUD'S THOUGHTS ON SEX & ORGASM

«The great question that has never been answered, and which I have not yet been able to answer, despite my thirty years of research into the feminine soul, is 'What does a woman want?'»

Sigmund Freud

From the beginning, *Freud* seemed to have an extremely "*friendly*" relationship with his sister-in-law, Minna Bernays, that had been engaged to one of *Freud's* friends, but the friend died of tuberculosis before they could marry. Even while *Freud* was chasing Martha and writing her love letters by the dozens telling her she was the love of his life; it seemed there could be no question about the one he was genuinely romancing.

Minna was brilliant, sarcastic, witty, and the so-called friendship she had with *Freud* maintained itself through all the years; they also lived in the same house for forty years. Minna even moved with *Freud's* family to London, which was not like *Freud's* sisters who he left behind. Freud and Minna took several trips together.

One could not help but think that it was weird that Minna's small bedroom was precisely next to Martha and *Sigmund's* bedroom, and they were only separated with a flimsy partition and no wall or door. Plus, the only way Minna could get to her bedroom was by walking through their bedroom.

We must remember that by the time Minna did move in, it was 1896, *Sigmund's* and *Martha's* sex life was over. Martha had decided she did not want to have more kids after they had six. *Freud* thought by using birth control might lead to a neurosis, so he quit having sex with his wife Martha, even though they kept sharing a bedroom.

Here is where it makes you wonder if he could tell the truth. *Freud* claimed that he was sexually abstinent after their children were born, even though he did hint there were some incidences of sex with Martha after the fact. He had written to his friend Fleiss that he dealt pretty often with impotence. (It is hard for this author to believe since that is all he thought about in some manner.)

≈

Before Minna had moved in, *Freud* did not claim to have been much of a sexual being. But, he sure had to have been a little interested to assist in giving birth to so many children.

≈

Freud respected and liked women; he seemed to have a series of powerful women friends, and amongst them '*Princess Marie Bonaparte*,' who had helped their entire family to escape from Vienna.

≈

When Anna, *Freud's* daughter, had become old enough to be his travel companion, then *Freud* started traveling with her. He seemed to enjoy talking to Minna of his ideas; as she appeared to understand them and was always supportive. It might have seemed sexist if he had left his wife and family at home and gone off with only his sister-in-law, but there is still a good chance that having sex did not have anything to do with the trips. And, whoever buys this malarkey, I have some oceanfront property to sell you in the middle of the United States.

≈

When accusing, *Freud* did '*wrench his patients*' medical histories from them and make them align with *Freud's* theories that could be pointed at the author, who pulled all the details of *Freud's* writings and doings into alignment with the theory of *Sigmund* to be an incompetent monster.

It had been deduced that while Freud's parents would go away and left *Freud* in charge of all his younger brothers and sisters, teenage *Freud* would sexually abuse his youngest sister. At the time *Freud* was in love with Martha, his mother, which he admitted later to one of his friends.

It was at that time that Wilhelm Fliess theorized that he had found in this case, with the phenomenon of what others called being in love with their mothers and jealous of their fathers, he now considered it to be a universal event that happened in everyone's early childhood if a male child.

Freud's ex-friends gave a damning verdict on him that when *Freud* said he was able to read others thoughts that he was only reading his thoughts into other people for their diagnoses.

Crews has been a one time friend of *Freud's* would like to

think that *Freud* had to have marred his aptitude even to be able to think straight. It was nothing for *Freud* to diagnose the patients he was treating with whatever 'ailment' *Freud* was currently causing him issues.

When a young female patient presented herself, by the name of Emma Eckstein, and she was complaining of her leg aching and painful periods. *Freud* eventually forced a story from her so it would fit his theory he was using at the time, and that was one when she had gotten mixed up with an erotic incident that had happened to her while still a virgin before she ever came into sexual awareness.

He felt all her problems had gotten suppressed so he could call it hysteria but was as if there were only a second incident that happened that brought the memory forth and caused everything to be horrifying.

Freud felt that if the patient never spoke of an erotic incident that happened before pubescent, then she or he had to be *'resistant.'* But *Freud* did not give up on his probing, and he finally got Emma to tell him that there had been a shop-keeper that had grabbed her genitals when she was only a child.

At that exact time, *Freud* hung on to that theory that one's nose was also the '*control center*' for all other organs in the body and their illnesses. He then took it on himself to give Emma a diagnosis. Not one but two syndromes, '*hystero-neurasthenia*,' with the neurosis part of it being brought on by one's masturbation.

～

Freud's treatment? To surgically remove a bone from poor Emma's nose was the recommended treatment. During that surgery, Emma hemorrhaged blood. Then, a month later, she had not quit bleeding, and it was still profusely that she did bleed. *Freud* told her family that all the bleeding was because she suffered from sexual longing – and her desires were being expressed when her blood spurted.

～

It was typical of *Freud*. He would go through a phase where he did "*pressure treatment*" on lady's bodies and foreheads inside his consulting room that he kept so dark. He would tell them to take off any tight clothes, and then he would search over their bodies for what he called their '*hystero-genic zones*,' while he would try to get them to tell him private details about their sexual history.

～

The more you read and research, it becomes more evident that there was one problem, and it was located inside *Freud's* head. Some called the inside of his head the "*his house of horrors*."

Freud thought that every boy was in love with their mommas, and they all wanted to kill their fathers, brought on by his Oedipus complex. He had a wild and weird theory about all women as being evil type creatures who had vaginas that were a threat to castrate any man who would cross its threshold.

Freud went on to state that every female had a secret ambition to gain an '***envied penis***' by cutting it off. Crews say that in *Freud's* mind, it would put together bizarre and illogic ideas along with desire, misogyny, and even cruelty.

Freud had another gift as well, and that was one of writing that would pull one in once they began reading what he had written. He used a lot of legendary situations so his prose would be more enhanced. You could always bet that the accounts that he wrote about of all his '***solved cases***' seemed to become popular because they turned out to be a mixture of what looked like detective stories and soft porn.

In some of *Freud's* writings, he would put down the questions he had asked his patient,

> *"Tell me, what part of his body were you able to feel that night?"*

Everyone who followed his writings like the nasty stuff he wrote and were exhilarated as they read quickly the accounts of the stimulating tension that went on between the patient and the analyst (*Freud*).

Freud was a professional at promoting himself; he could bribe himself to be a professor at the Vienna University, *Freud* was like a parasite and would latch on to theories of others and later he would condemn those same people that had helped him get ahead.

It was a real pity that *Freud's* wife, Martha, had been so playful, sweet, ardent, and a young woman who *Freud* could slowly extinguish her personality. It could be seen in the self-obsessed letters (almost narcissistic) letters, he would write to Martha during the entire four years they were engaged, and while he was working to succeed at being successful. You could read common words and signs of what one now could call coercive control.

Freud worked to cut her away from her friends and her family and get her to pull away from her Orthodox Jewish faith to which she had always been so faithful.

Freud told Martha in one of the letters that he had been unbearable recently, question yourself what has made me this way. Gee, what a way to manipulate someone, would you not say?

After Martha had given birth to *Freud's* six children, her figure was gone, and he saw her as the one used up woman. He could not accept growing old with her but expected her body to stay the way it was when he was dating her. Their sex life was over, and it seems that was when *Freud* started his sexual affair with Martha's sister, Minna, who had come to live with them after she had become widowed.

Sigmund had a theory on Vaginal Orgasm

By no means did *Sigmund Freud's* idea about this cause any revelation, but it started a new debate that still rages today. A new genetics study and a book written on how the female orgasm has evolved might help make one understand this complicated reflex that seemed to make women feel so good and much happier.

Freud's idea was that for the female to have pleasure and to feel an orgasm that it should be centered '*on*' the ladies reproductive tract. *Freud* knew that many women had experienced orgasm through a small organ that was called the clitoris, but he said that orgasms from the clitoris were only "*infantile*." He said that if a woman could not move her '*center*' of sensitivity to her vagina, then she should have the label as frigid. That idea alone caused thousands of fake orgasms.

When you research sex, you will find that almost always 95% of men will have an orgasm from intercourse while women will only reach about 25 – 30%. (So hard to imagine!) There are 30% more of women who have NEVER had an orgasm during intercourse, (how sad for them) and then a 30-40% say they have had them sometimes. (What is this world coming to? Seriously? Where did this "*data*" come from?) Some women have multiple orgasms in one intercourse session. (Happy are they!) Then there is Tantric sex that assists the male or female to enjoy much longer orgasms. One could go on and on, but you can see where sex has come from since *Freud* thought he knew so much about the topic.

There was another study from a hospital in London that also said there was wide variation in women with their tendencies in orgasms and it was traced not to be so neurotic as *Freud* had wanted it to be, but the real blame was to be genetics.

Freud after theorizing much, eventually said that female sexuality should be called the "*Dark Continent*," implying he did not understand any of this. One must wonder if *Martha Freud* would have admitted to faking her orgasms or if she ever had felt an orgasm.

PART XI

AFTER FREUD'S DEATH

«A civilization which leaves so large a number of its participants unsatisfied and drives them into revolt neither has nor deserves the prospect of a lasting existence.»

Sigmund Freud

As we look back and realize how long *Freud* has been dead, it seems so strange that his '***provocative theories***' remain in some discussions today in neuroscience, culture, and psychology despite his ideas being mind-boggling and catastrophically WRONG.

So why will he NOT go away? No matter if you hate the man or love him, you can't deny that *Freud* made himself a giant in his field even if he was a fraud. When you think about the influence he had on psychoanalysis, psychology, all our theories of mind, he has been and will be given credit for kindling a revolution.

~

Freud's legacy has come thru the ages and his ideas as crazy as they are have permeated into Western culture. There is rarely a day that someone somewhere does not utter one of his terms: arrested development, mommy and daddy issues, *Freudian* slips, death wishes, anal retentiveness, cathartic release, phallic symbols, defense mechanisms and on and on and on.

~

His legacy today is now a shaky one, and he has lost all favor in academia. There is almost no institution that would use him to be a credible source. As far as *Freud* being a research paradigm, it is all dead.

~

Freud's theory on female sexuality and his thoughts regarding homosexuality are for sure reviled, that cause many feminists to call him a different kind of "*F*" word. Some argue he should be spelled "*Fraud*" and not "*Freud*."

~

It can for sure be said that there was no other notable figure in all of history who was so obviously wrong about everything he said. But, you know, academia is very creative to whitewash *Freud's* errors, while the lay reader will become dumbfounded by the mess *Freud* left behind.

FREUDIAN MISCONCEPTIONS

The main problem with *Freud*, that even while some of his ideas might have appeared to be intriguing, there was almost no evidence in backing them up. Modern psychology has not been able to substantiate any of his claims.

THERE WAS no scientific evidence that supported *Freud's* idea that boys lusted after their Moms and hated their Fathers. He was so messed up, and so utterly wrong when it came to gender. When the idea of "*penis envy*" now comes up, it is laughed at, and everyone feels it tragic.

FREUD HAD THEORIZED that someone who was a homosexual was a failure to be able to resolve the patient's anal phase.

He argued that there would only be "*mature*" women who could obtain an orgasm when they had vaginal sex. Those women who were only able to climax by clitoral stimulation were stunted or stuck into a latent phase. Once again, more of his nonsense.

FREUD DEVELOPED an abnormal growth in his mouth that would be later diagnosed as cancer of the soft palate. He waited several years before seeing a doctor because he, Dr. *Freud*, was already sure it was cancer, and it would be blamed on his cigars.

WHEN DEUTSCH LOOKED AT CANCER, he said the first glance told him there was no doubt it was advanced cancer. But he gave himself some extra time by looking at *Freud's* mouth again and decided to diagnose it as a case of leukoplakia brought on by excessive smoking.

BUT, as everyone knew, it was not leukoplakia; in fact, it was a pre-cancerous lesion. Deutsch knew as soon as he saw it that it was cancer. Doctors of that time usually concealed if there was a "*bad*" diagnosis for the patient.

DEUTSCH IMMEDIATELY WAS able to tell the type of cancer he

was dealing with, but on the other hand, he did not size up *Freud* correctly.

DEUTSCH HAD ONLY LATELY WATCHED *Freud* as he had suffered such intense grief after his six-year-old grandson died from TB, and Deutsch said he was afraid if he told *Freud* the real diagnosis that it might throw *Freud* into a heart attack.

FREUD HAD ASKED Deutsch if he would be willing to help him leave this world if his suffering became unbearable if he would help him slip from this world with dignity.

DR. DEUTSCH'S WIFE, Helene, remembered that her husband finally came home after *Freud's* first surgery and stayed alone until the wee hours of the morning before he finally came out and talked to her. He told her that he would no longer be *Freud's* doctor as he had lost *Freud's* confidence. *Freud* had grown angry because Deutsch had not believed he had enough strength to hear the real diagnosis.

IN 1926 THERE was a new doctor who had started giving medical care to Princess Marie Bonaparte, who was in Vienna being analyzed by *Freud*. The princess finally suggested for Schur to be *Freud's* new physician. Even though throughout his years with cancer, *Freud* suffered through over 30 different surgeries from it.

His cancer remained stable until it turned 1936, and then there were new malignant tumors that were spreading on the palate of his mouth. 1937 saw more cancer and more procedures. In 1938 the time came when part of cancer could not be reached. It was all downhill now. However, in 1939, they did try radiation on cancer.

Freud's condition was deteriorating quickly, and Dr. Schur decided to move into *Freud's* house with him. *Freud* had a pet dog that he loved and adored, but the smell of necrotic bone coming from *Freud's* jaw. It was so repulsive that the dog could not stand to be in the room with his master. Last six months, *Freud* was confined to bed and dependent on the care of others.

There had been periods that *Freud* had to wear a hideous looking, prosthesis that was denture-like so he could keep his nasal and oral cavities separated, but the device kept him from speaking and eating normally. It was after his first surgeries in 1923 that he had become deaf in the right ear.

September 21ST, *Freud* reminded Schur of their talk the first time they met and the promise that had been made when the time came. He then told that he was in constant pain and torture, and it made no sense now.

SCHUR ASSURED *Freud* that he had not forgotten and *Freud* was relieved and asked for his daughter Anna be told. He was fully aware of what he was asking.

WHEN *FREUD* WAS AGAIN in agony, Schur gave him two cms of morphine. *Freud* soon was feeling relief and went into a very peaceful sleep. His facial expression of suffering and pain was gone. In twelve hours, the dose was repeated. *Freud* lapsed into a coma and didn't wake up again.

IT WAS three in the early morning September 23rd, 1939, 75 years ago when *Freud* died quietly. It would be three days later when they would cremate his body. They placed his ashes in a chosen ancient Greek urn which had been a gift from Marie Bonaparte. *Freud* had left his pocket watch to Schur who passed it on down through his children and then their children.

PART XII

CONCLUSION

The Good, The Bad, and The Ugly About Sigmund Freud

Good Points

- Honestly, few he seemed to have in this author's opinion. But, one must admit he was a genius; possibly even had a high IQ.
- It seems that his research abilities were remarkable before he became so enthralled with sex.
- He did explore the possibilities of good uses for cocaine for his patients as well as himself.

Bad Points

- He was nothing but a pervert, and in this day he would be in prison for molesting his daughter over and over.
- Deserting his wife and turning to his sister-in-law for sex after his wife had their sixth child.
- He put on the airs that he was better and smarter than anyone else.
- He was nothing but a quack in his time; that has taken decades to prove.
- He was a full out narcissist.
- Cocaine addict, not just carrying out research, but an addict.

Only in the opinion of this writer of course; but *Freud* living did not leave a tremendous mark on this world. He traumatized so many women and those he did not traumatize he messed their heads up so bad they never knew what normal was for the rest of their lives.

It is too bad that someone that could have helped the world so much with his intelligence could, in turn, cause so much harm.

Being a narcissist, of course, *Freud* never thought of anyone but himself, himself, himself. He dressed impeccably and made sure he was able to keep up with 20 cigars a day habit which would eventually bring him death.

So, is this author sad that *Freud* is no longer used in colleges around the world? Absolutely not! Am I happy that physicians are now much smarter and laughing at him and all his '*discoveries*.' You bet!

PART XIII

FURTHER READING

- The Basic Writings of Sigmund Freud
  (Psychopathology of Everyday Life, the
  Interpretation of Dreams, and Three
  Contributions To the Theory of Sex) by Sigmund
  Freud and A.A. Brill – July 10, 1995.
- The Future of An Illusion (The Standard Edition)
  (Complete Psychological Works of Sigmund
  Freud) by Sigmund Freud, James Strachey, et al. –
  September 17th, 1989.
- Sexuality and The Psychology of Love by
  Sigmund Freud – April 1, 1997.

YOUR FREE EBOOK!

As a way of saying thank you for reading our book, we're offering you a free copy of the below eBook.

Happy Reading!

GO WWW.THEHISTORYHOUR.COM/CLEO/